IMAGES
*of America*

# DAYTON'S
# DEPARTMENT STORE

*On the cover:* Nicollet Avenue and Seventh Street are pictured here on November 25, 1948, the busiest shopping day of the year, the day after Thanksgiving. A vibrant downtown Minneapolis is alive with Christmas spirit, many shoppers are heading for Dayton's. (Courtesy of Target.)

IMAGES
*of America*

# DAYTON'S
# DEPARTMENT STORE

*Best wishes,*

*M. Firestone*

Mary Firestone

ARCADIA
PUBLISHING

Copyright © 2007 by Mary Firestone
ISBN 978-0-7385-5061-9

Published by Arcadia Publishing
Charleston SC, Chicago IL, Portsmouth NH, San Francisco CA

Printed in the United States of America

Library of Congress Catalog Card Number: 2007925088

For all general information contact Arcadia Publishing at:
Telephone 843-853-2070
Fax 843-853-0044
E-mail sales@arcadiapublishing.com
For customer service and orders:
Toll-Free 1-888-313-2665

Visit us on the Internet at www.arcadiapublishing.com

# CONTENTS

# ACKNOWLEDGMENTS

I gratefully acknowledge Dayton's for all it has given the citizens of Minnesota. I also want to thank Target, the Minnesota Historical Society, and the Minneapolis Public Library for their role in this project. I also wish to thank my family for their love and support.

Unless otherwise indicated, all photographs are courtesy of Target.

# INTRODUCTION

When George Draper Dayton first stepped off the train onto Minnesota land in 1881, he arrived at a time when the prairie was alive with Native American tribes, herds of bison, and rich, unbroken soil. He came because of investments he made in the area around Worthington, an interest he shared with several other eastern investors who had lent money to the wave of European immigrants needing cash to settle in the Midwest. But their investments were destabilized by draught, grasshopper plagues, and extreme winters, making life difficult if not impossible for settlers to make a living from their farms, and many abandoned their land. Their mortgages had been managed locally, but Dayton got involved directly when settlers defaulted. Frequently he helped them get back on their feet.

Dayton clearly had financial reasons to settle in the area, but having grown up in a small town in rural New York, he was drawn to the prairie. He built a large home in Worthington, bought the town bank, and his young family soon joined him. He also formed the Minnesota Loan and Investment Company, and the success of that company eventually made it necessary for Dayton to explore other ways to put his money to work.

After carefully researching the potential of different cities, Dayton decided on the commercial promise of Minneapolis, which was already booming with the lumber and flour mills of St. Anthony. When Westminster Presbyterian church, which was on the southwest corner of Nicollet Avenue and Seventh Street, burned to the ground, he bought the land. He put up a new building on the property and was looking around for tenants when two young businessmen came to him for a loan. They said they wanted to buy a clothing store down the street called Goodfellow's.

Dayton loaned them the money and became a silent partner in the process. He then convinced the partners to relocate, making Goodfellow's a tenant in his new building at Nicollet Avenue and Seventh Street. Soon the store's name was changed from Goodfellow's to Dayton's Daylight Store, and when George Dayton became the sole owner in 1903, the name was changed to Dayton Dry Goods Company. The business had its struggles in the first years, because Dayton had never been a merchant. However, the retail bug must have bit hard, because he became extremely determined despite all the losses, saying, "I kept track of the losses until they passed one hundred thousand dollars," adding, "we're going to make this a win."

Dayton Dry Goods occupied three floors of a new, six-story building and was remarkable in the day for its roominess and large windows. The first floor ceilings were 16 feet high, and daylight flooded the space because in those days, there were very few tall buildings nearby to block its flow. At night, incandescent globes cast a warm glow, reflecting highly polished glass and wood cabinets filled with exquisite linens, stockings, petticoats, gloves, notions, and perfumes. As the store expanded every few years, comforts were increased. Restrooms were added to every floor, as well as escalators and new services such as the Looking Glass Salon and an infirmary. A soda fountain and lunchroom were added to the Downstairs Store (also known as the basement store), which in its day was the third largest retail outlet in the Twin Cities, fulfilling George Dayton's wish to make the store accessible to as many people as possible.

Donaldsons' Glass Block occupied the southeast corner of Nicollet Avenue and Sixth Street, and the proximity of the two stores led to a race (or a war, as the *Minneapolis Tribune* described it at the time) for the largest Nicollet Avenue presence, with Dayton's emerging as the winner in 1917. This was no small feat considering Donaldsons' equally elegant merchandise and interior, plus a two-decade lead in retail. But Dayton, determined to lead, caught the eye of consumers with promotions, sales, and over-the-top publicity moves. In 1920, he hired Curtiss Northwest Airplane Company to fly merchandise from New York, with a dramatic landing in Minneapolis's Parade Stadium. The de Havilland planes were then steered through the streets (with wings removed) arriving at Nicollet Avenue and Seventh Street, where the pilot handed over boxes of goods with flight goggles still on his head. It was the longest commercial flight on record at over 1,600 miles.

Dayton said his experience as a banker was invaluable to the survival of the store. Certainly his considerable wealth did not hurt either, since he could absorb losses, learn lessons, and begin again. His eldest son, Draper, is noted in the store's history for his leadership and intuitive sense as a merchant and was a major force in the store's success. Even though he was a Princeton University graduate, he chose to work his way up through each department before taking over as general manager in 1911. Like his father, Draper enjoyed analyzing aspects of their business. After spending time in the leading New York department stores, he discovered that "the biggest factor in the success of the best stores is a different atmosphere, a personality which pervades the whole store and must come from the top." He added, "We are in a position to give that and we must do it." Draper understood that the way to acquire this atmosphere was through a spirit of service, enthusiasm, and good will, all of which spread throughout the company and ultimately to the community at large.

After Draper took over as manager in 1911, his brother Nelson joined the firm, owning a portion equal to Draper's. Nelson had spent many years running a farm in Anoka County, a life he found satisfying, but Draper and George continued to ask him to join in the business. He eventually acquiesced, and Dayton's then officially became a family business.

The success of the store was extraordinary, but Dayton's was not without its difficult times. A fire destroyed a large section of the store on a bitterly cold February night in 1917. In 1923, Draper suddenly died of heart failure, devastating the family and the business. Two other key managers had died the year before, and a heartsick George Dayton wanted to sell. However, Nelson urged his father to stay with it for two or three years to see how it went, and George finally agreed.

Nelson then launched a nationwide executive search, assembling a team whose collective experience gave Dayton's all it needed to move forward. His leadership was shared by the knowledgeable executive team, and George, who always remained president of the firm, kept his office on the fourth floor and, as always, walked to work every day. Even though it had been severely shaken, Dayton's department store steadied itself and began again.

Throughout his life, George was a deeply religious man, who kept the Sabbath. Like many stores of the day, Dayton's was closed on Sundays, but he insisted on keeping the Sabbath strictly and refused to advertise in the Sunday papers. Even the Christmas lights were dark on Sundays. When he died in 1938, Nelson took over as president and made his share of changes, but he always upheld the restriction of Sunday advertising. Dayton's did not advertise on Sundays until 1954, three years after Nelson's death.

During Nelson's time as president, more family members entered the fold. His eldest son, Donald, had already started in 1937, one year before George Dayton died. By the late 1940s, all five of Nelson's sons had joined the firm: Bruce Dayton in 1940, Wallace and Kenneth Dayton in 1946, and Douglas in 1948. With all the "Mr. Daytons" in the store, employees simplified things by attaching "Mr." to their first names, calling them Mr. Nelson, Mr. Bruce, Mr. Kenneth, Mr. Wallace, Mr. Douglas, and Mr. Donald.

The decade of the 1940s marked a period of extraordinary growth for Dayton's with a $1.5 million expansion that raised all but the Nicollet Avenue and Seventh Street buildings to 12 stories and added air conditioning throughout the whole store. In 1943, the Model Room was renamed the Oval Room and, per the expansion, was remodeled again in 1947.

Minneapolis was the "fashion center of the northwest" in the 1940s, considered by Minnesota retailers to be second to none in the world. Fashion shows were a daily occurrence at the best Nicollet Avenue stores, and Dayton's eighth floor in particular was the place to go, where models paraded the best and the latest designs for the fashion conscious. Everyone downtown was fashion conscious.

Spring flower shows became a part of Dayton's in the 1930s, and in the 1960s, the store joined with Bachman's Florists to create public events on the eighth floor, providing a much needed respite for winter-weary Minnesotans. In earlier years, flowers filled the aisles on the main floor of the Minneapolis store, often eclipsing the products and display cases.

"Daytonia," the youthful, vibrant source of the company's esprit de corps, worked and played together around the clock, especially during the first few decades of the store's life. The biweekly *Daytonews* delivered store business, photograph essays, sales reports, cartoons, and fatherly wisdom from the pen of George Dayton. The quiet pace of each issue reflected the small-town atmosphere of the store, a world in itself. In its carefree expression of the lives of employees, at work and personal adventures in equal measure, *Daytonews* belied the vigor of Dayton's growth and ambition, a store that was reaching to the sky from nearly every corner of the block. Dayton's also had significant involvement in the Minneapolis Aquatennial each year, with spectacular floats and store competitions for Queen of the Lakes candidates. Issues of *Daytonews* were often filled with photographs and long stories about the candidates and the competition.

Throughout its existence, Dayton's was always focused on increasing the comfort and pleasure of its patrons, evidenced by the expanding tearooms, which evolved from the small, quaint spaces for a few shoppers, to the soaring 12th floor Sky Room of the 1920s, with its panoramic views of Downtown Minneapolis. It was grand with Czechoslovakian chandeliers, yellow, grey, and gold decor, and concealed colored lights that provided colorful, delicate "paintings" on the walls.

Among the most memorable events at Dayton's were the promotions and Christmas window displays. In the 1920s, a few displays were dramatic to the extreme, with live tigers and bears, to the surprise and delight of pedestrians strolling by. One year, two bears broke out of a confined window space and wreaked havoc in the store before they were finally caught. The displays were tamed down somewhat in later years, but still drew crowds five and six deep, gathering at the windows to watch the magic of Christmas come alive once more at Dayton's. Later years brought the extremely popular Santa Bear, Willy Wonka, and Paddington Bear exhibits. Santa Bear was especially popular, causing a few upsets when their numbers dwindled at some locations.

The 1960s and 1970s brought new fashion trends, reflecting a public less focused on solid, timeless design. Dayton's Out of Sight and Indeed! shops maximized the store's role in the trend market, providing younger shoppers a concentration of all that was new and hip. Fashion designers were enjoying rock star status during the 1960s, touring the nation and making appearances at the Minneapolis Dayton's. Yves Saint Laurent, Geoffrey Beene, Bill Blass, and the English fashion model Twiggy all made stops at Dayton's. Kenneth Dayton was the general manager of the store during this phase, and his "Youthquakes" drew crowds to the store for weekly concerts, drawing 130,000 people to the Minneapolis store in just eight days. Needless to say, sales reflected it.

The 1960s and 1970s marked another period of expansion for Dayton's, beginning with the merger with Hudson's of Detroit, which formed the Dayton Hudson Corporation. The "Dales," Brookdale, Ridgedale, Rosedale, sprawled at the edges of the Twin Cities metropolitan area after the extraordinary success of Southdale. Each mall was owned by Dayton's and each had a Dayton's flagship store. Dayton's also rebuilt the former Schuneman's space in St. Paul, and eventually built stores all over the Midwest, some of them in malls, others as stand-alone businesses.

In the 1980s, Dayton's formed a new kind of relationship with Hudson's of Detroit. After operating independently for many years, the two companies combined to form the Dayton Hudson Department Store Company, making it the largest department store company in America. In 1987, its annual sales were $1.5 billion from 37 stores in seven Midwestern states. At that time, Dayton's had 17 stores in Minnesota, North Dakota, South Dakota, and Wisconsin, and Hudson's had 20 stores in Michigan, Indiana, and Ohio.

Dayton's purchased Marshall Field's in 1990 and, in 2001, all of Dayton's stores were renamed Marshall Field's.

Nostalgic shoppers can still (as of this book's publication) visit the original Dayton's building at 700 on the Mall, and ride the escalators up to the Sky Room and Oak Grille restaurants, which are busy as ever on the 12th floor, now a Macy's. A small history museum of Dayton's, Hudson's, and Marshall Field's remains in place outside the doors for the Oak Grille. If one tries, one might still feel the magic of Dayton's when reading about its past.

The images in this book focus on the Minneapolis Dayton's, its early developments, departments, and fashion through the years.

# One

# BEFORE 1920

Before George Dayton invested in downtown Minneapolis, he spent time on the city's street corners paying close attention to how many people were passing by. He also kept an office in the Kasota Building at Hennepin Avenue and Fourth Street, where he thoroughly researched the local market and the future of Minneapolis. After a year of careful consideration, he began buying along Nicollet Avenue, limiting himself to the area between Fourth and Tenth Streets. Although local business people considered this land too far north of Bridge Square to be viable commercial property, Dayton's keen instinct and research told him otherwise. This early-1900s street scene along Nicollet Avenue between Sixth and Seventh Streets shows a sidewalk crowded with shoppers and pedestrians, similar to what Dayton, at age 39, might have observed. (Courtesy of the Minnesota Historical Society.)

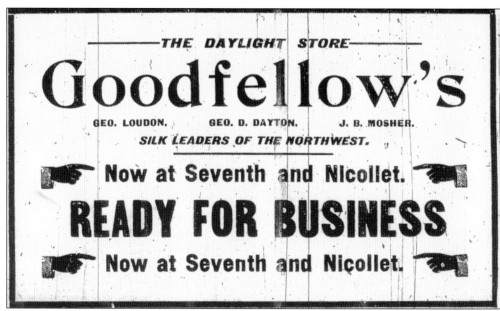

In June 1902, this Goodfellow's advertisement appeared in the *Minneapolis Journal* without the Dayton name. In subsequent years, the Dayton name appeared with greater prominence as George Dayton took over the business, eventually buying out his two partners, while increasing the responsibilities of his eldest son, Draper. On opening day, the store occupied three floors of the available six, with 20 departments consisting of silks, woolens, petticoats, ribbons, rugs, and draperies. (Courtesy of the Minneapolis Library archives.)

In June 1903, this *Minneapolis Tribune* advertisement appeared, announcing the transition from Goodfellow's to Dayton's. Draper Dayton's name appears, indicating his new role in the store. George's connection to Worthington is also noted as a "former" home base, indicating his commitment to the urban real estate of Minneapolis and retail. Later the store name would be changed again to Dayton Dry Goods Company and, after that, the Dayton Company. (Courtesy of the Minneapolis Library archives.)

This is Dayton's as it appeared in its first days with the Goodfellow's sign still intact, but this was removed the following year. George bought out his partners, and changed the store's name from Dayton's Daylight Store to Dayton Dry Goods Company on May 18, 1903.

This image captures a bustling mix of pedestrians and horse-drawn carts at Nicollet Avenue and Seventh Street around 1902, with the Dayton's sign in the background looking thoroughly modern. The six-story structure was built on the former site of the Westminster Presbyterian church, which burned to the ground years before. In its early years, Dayton's employed 240 people in a wide range of jobs, from candymakers and bakers, to buyers whose trips to Paris brought Minneapolis the latest in haute couture. (Courtesy of the Minnesota Historical Society.)

In this display window, Dayton's shows Edwardian-style dresses, which were very fashionable in the early 1900s. Complex in their construction and expensive, this century-old silhouette left the fashion scene forever at the start of World War I, making way for simpler styles and ready-to-wear clothes that were available to everyone.

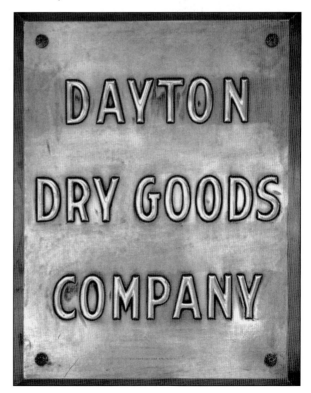

This was the Dayton Dry Goods Company cornerstone plaque in 1903.

In a 1903 *Minneapolis Journal* advertisement, Dayton's offered common stock to employees and the public at $100 a share, an idea George Dayton adopted from European cooperative retailers. He was quoted in the *Minneapolis Journal*, saying, "I believe in the cultivation of the most kindly feeling between the firm and its employees. If we give the employees this opportunity it will cement pleasant relations."

16

In this 1909 Dayton's postcard advertisement, American Lady brand corsets are featured. Beneath this extravagantly appointed La Belle Epoque dress, the corset created the S-bend silhouette this era was known for. Miss Helen, a well known Minneapolis dressmaker who made complex and elaborate gowns for the city's society women, had a shop in Dayton's that drew customers who could put such products to good use.

Dayton's display window shows 1900s Edwardian beachwear in dark colors, the latest in warm weather fashion. The suits were made of wool bloomers and jackets and were not complete without stockings, hats, and footwear.

FASHION'S FAVORITE SILKS FOR SHIRTWAIST SUITS AND COATS

| | | |
|---|---|---|
| TWILLED FOULARDS | BLACK PONGEES | NEW BEYADERE EFFECTS—many good colors |
| SWISS HABUTAIS—absolutely spot proof | CLOTHS OF GOLD   CLOTHS OF SILVER | SATIN IMPRIME FOULARDS |
| NATURAL PONGEE—Real Shantung, all grades | NEW NOVELTY TAFFETA | BLACK INDIAS—27 and 36 inches wide |
| REAL SHANTUNG PONGEE—fifteen wanted colors | SATIN BROCHE FOULARDS—exclusive designs | AJAX  BLACK  TAFFETAS |
| TWENTY-FOUR INCH POPLINS—extra fine | JACQUARD CHECKED TAFFETA—very natty | WHITE PONGEES—wash beautifully |
| PEAU de CREPE—for which we are agents | HAIRLINE STRIPES—with swivel dot and figure | SMALL TASTY EFFECTS IN BLACK—very late arrivals |
| CREPE de CHINE—queen of light dress fabrics | OLGA CLOTHS—fifteen good colors | VOILES—forty-five inches wide |

With direct-mail advertisements in 1904, Dayton Dry Goods both educates and tantalizes customers, describing the many uses for the varieties of colorful silks available to them. John Per-Lee relished his job as Dayton's buyer of silks and laces, "in an era when fabulous quantities of goods were required to properly drape the human form divine," writes Dayton's historian James Gray in *You Can Get it At Dayton's*. That year, Dayton's offered 100,000 yards in its annual silk and velvet sale, making it necessary to move other departments around to accommodate the volume. The finest fabrics had names such as Ombre velvets, panne velvets, Peau de Cynge silks, lumineaux, and Pompadour silks. Per-Lee's ambition for silks is considered a source of the store's early success.

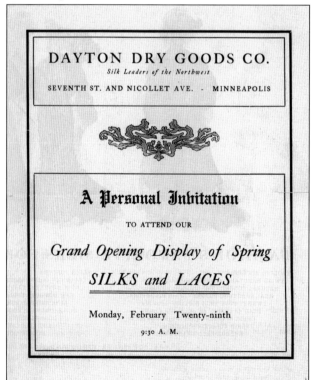

Dayton Dry Goods sent this personal invitation to attend their grand opening display of spring featuring silks and laces in 1904.

In this 1911 postcard advertisement, Dayton's illustrates shipments of merchandise by air and by sea. A note on the other side from the buyers describes the breadth of their purchases, from Paris couture to Irish linens, all for the Dayton's shopper, of course.

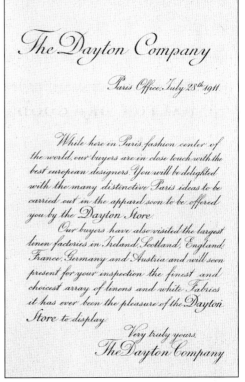

The Dayton Company

Paris Office, July 28th 1911

While here in Paris, fashion center of the world, our buyers are in close touch with the best european designers. You will be delighted with the many distinctive Paris ideas to be carried out in the apparel soon to be offered you by the Dayton Store.

Our buyers have also visited the largest linen factories in Ireland, Scotland, England, France, Germany and Austria and will soon present for your inspection the finest and choicest array of linens and white Fabrics it has ever been the pleasure of the Dayton Store to display.

Very truly yours,
The Dayton Company

Dayton's advertises a Saturday After Supper Sale in 1911, encouraging customers to head downtown even if it is late, to take advantage of prices on crockery, home furnishings, and kitchen utensils, possibly in the bargain basement. In those days, the basement store had no regular stock of its own but instead consisted of discontinued items from upstairs departments.

In the first decade of the 20th century, the *Daytona* brought goods across Lake Minnetonka to homes along the shore during the summer.

During the second decade of the 20th century, Dayton's fabrics and notions department, with elegant light fixtures and cream color ceilings, offset the dark display tables and (dusty) flooring. Each of the large columns in Dayton's main store were made of concrete and steel and were well anchored at 55 feet below street level.

1. Don't make a practice of coming late to business. It's more to your interest to come a few minutes early.
2. Don't dress dowdily, gaudily or dudishly, but cleanly, neatly and nicely.
3. Don't wait upon customers with your hands dirty or your finger nails in mourning.
4. Don't manicure your nails during business hours.
5. Don't forget it doesn't cost a cent to be a mannerly man or a womanly woman.
6. Don't address a customer as "Lady." Madam is the proper term, or say "Gents' goods." "Men's goods" is better.
7. Don't leave your department except in the interest of the business.
8. Don't allow dirt or disorder in your stock. Keep store as a good housekeeper would keep house.
9. Don't dust your goods or counters aisle ward while customers are passing.
10. Don't allow a customer to look in vain for somebody to wait upon her while you are engaged in talking to your fellow clerk about last evening's experiences.
11. Don't get excited in times of a rush or any other time; it shows the customer that you are inexperienced and unaccustomed to an active business.
12. Don't chase customers! wait till they stop and show that they are interested in goods or some department, then approach them in a business-like manner.
13. Don't greet your customer with a beer, tobacco or onion breath. It hastens them to move on to more fragrant surroundings. No danger if you don't in
14. Don't chew gum or tobacco.
15. Don't be disloyal to your employer.
16. Don't indulge in gossip.
17. Don't be discourteous to customers. It's a fault which cannot be excused.
18. Don't stand and stare at customers, or make remarks or criticisms in regard to the style or color of their dress.
19. Don't laugh loudly or use slang phrases.
20. Don't congregate and visit.
21. Don't stand in a listless manner while customers are examining goods—be attentive, and show an interest in your employer's business.
22. Don't forget that being absent from your department in the basement or elsewhere decreases the amount of your sales.
23. Don't always show the cheapest goods first. Sales are sometimes lost that way.
24. Don't fail to remember that it is for your interest as well as your employers', for you to take short lunch hours on busy days.
25. Don't fail to remember that customers frequently hand you a $2.00 bill, and when you hand them the change declare they gave you a $5.00 bill. Call back the amount every time. It's easy when you get used to it.
26. Don't borrow lead pencils or scissors from one another.
27. Don't swing or twirl your scissors, lead pencil or other tools of trade.
28. Don't lose your check books for one minute.
29. Don't make out a sales check without fully itemizing it, and write plainly.

COPYRIGHT BY O. N. POWELL

# STORE DON'TS

Always be prepared to produce this booklet when called for

30. Don't take an address for goods to be sent a C. O. D. order or a charge without being positive that you take it correctly.
31. Don't forget that no sales means no profit or that upon the amount of your sales, to a great extent, depends the amount of your salary.
32. Don't misrepresent goods. You can sell more without. "A pleased customer, always a customer."
33. Don't fail to know what goods are in your stock, and where to find them quickly.
34. Don't underestimate the real worth of a customer to your employer. Sometimes a good customer indirectly pays your salary.
35. Don't permit a customer to leave a department dissatisfied or offended, before sending for some one in higher authority.
36. Don't be so persistent in your efforts to make a sale, that you make yourself objectionable to your customer.
37. Don't give an inch over-measure or an eighth of an inch short measure.
38. Don't argue or contend with business associates in the presence of customers.
39. Don't permit envy or unfriendliness to exist between you and other employes. Best results are obtained by concerted action.
40. Don't disregard instructions from those holding superior positions.
41. Don't think all customers are honest or give might-be thieves a chance to steal.
42. Don't write notes or read papers, books or letters during business hours.
43. Don't be an eye servant. Be a faithful co-worker in sight or out of sight.

44. Don't expect an increased salary from any source but faithful and valuable service.
45. Don't let false pride hinder you from doing honest labor.
46. Don't think you are not appreciated if you are worthy. When business justifies it you'll share in the benefit.
47. Don't say "I was not hired to do that.". It might cost you your situation and reference to obtain another.
48. Don't delude yourself by thinking you are deluding your employer, if he does not constantly call your attention to your business faults.
49. Don't lose sight of the fact that your record is as much to you as your salary —sometimes more.
50. Don't misuse privileges. There is someone who appreciates fair treatment waiting for your situation.
51. Don't be afraid of making suggestions for the betterment of the business. If heard from it is a sign that you are using your eyes and ears to advantage.
52. Don't promenade the aisles arm in arm. This is a habit employes occasionally fall into when meeting by chance on store business errands.
53. Don't ask after a customer is through making a purchase, "Is that all?" The customer may think her purchase is considered too small, but ask, "Is there anything else you wish?" or "Is there anything else I can show you?"
54. Don't send a customer to any part of the store for goods called for unless you are sure they will be found in the place as directed.
55. Don't "hum" or "whistle" in a department or at a desk, it annoys customers and aggravates your business associates.
56. Don't say of goods asked for and not in stock that same are not made—you might be mistaken.
57. Don't disparage other stores or people connected with same. Keep silent rather than make any uncomplimentary remarks of business neighbors.
58. Don't allow yourself to become irritable because some customers occasionally detain you a few minutes after doors close.
59. Don't promise "special delivery" without first consulting proper authority.
60. Don't tell a customer that goods on display in windows are not for sale.
61. Don't entertain those who seek social visits—social visits from friends are not proper during business hours.
62. Don't accept a position unless you are perfectly willing and anxious to follow the rules of the store in every detail pleasantly and efficiently.
63. Don't try to substitute anything for tact, push and principle.

Don't mislay, destroy, or fail to read these "Store Don'ts"—preserve them—re-read them—think about them—act upon them. You'll never be out of employment if you do.

Employes' business capital is knowledge of facts herein contained, and performance of the same.

This little booklet is the outgrowth of observation and practical experience.

**DAYTON DRY GOODS CO.,**

In this 1905 issue of *Daytonews*, store management makes it clear how employees should act.

This 1913 Dayton's advertisement ran in the *Minneapolis Journal* for its 11th anniversary sale. In a tiered format, the illustration depicts the stages of Dayton's growth. By 1913, a new annex had begun to include a subbasement, and one new store structure along the rear of the original building, creating an entrance along Eighth Street.

Here is a 1910 art gallery at Dayton's, possibly Beard's, which was one among several departments leased to outside vendors in the first store. Dayton's later absorbed all of the departments. Beard's Gallery consisted of seven rooms and displayed works from Paris, Boston, and the Library of Congress. Other leased departments were Gertrude Stanton's optical service, Read's drawing supplies, and W. B. Sayre's hardware, china, and glassware.

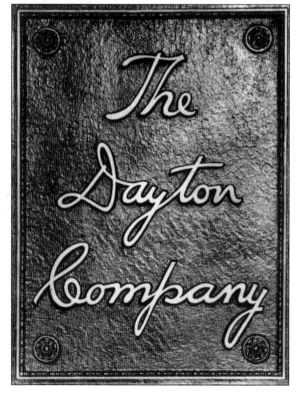

When the store's corporate name was changed from Dayton Dry Goods Company to the Dayton Company in 1911, a new plaque replaced the old at Nicollet Avenue and Seventh Street.

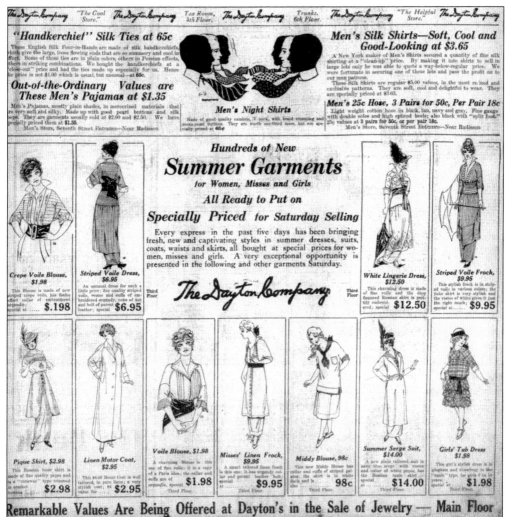

In an elaborately illustrated 1914 newspaper advertisement, Dayton's shows summer garments for "women, misses, and girls." Dayton's ready-to-wear departments were growing, and their success was attributed to the team philosophy adopted by Draper Dayton and George Dayton, who assembled a group of talented merchandisers eager to share their expertise, yet work together. This team approach remained a foundation of Dayton's. The original group consisted of Charles J. Larson, John Per-Lee, and John Luker.

**Vol. III., No. 12.**     Minneapolis, December 30, 1919     **Price 2 Cents**

## THE NEW YEAR

Happy New Year to every one in Daytonia.

That is the hearty wish of each member of the firm for you all. What is 1920 going to bring to us as individuals?

Whatever of trial or disappointment comes, let us meet it cheerfully with brave hearts and smiling faces.

In the prayer nearly all of us have said daily since childhood, we ask God to "give us this day our daily bread"—that means we ask Him to give us strength for all the experiences of daily life.

It is fortunate we cannot see into the future. Going forward day by day, only a day at a time, we pass on through the years finding our strength strengthened by the Source of all real help, equal to the necessities. So may it be to all of you this 1920 and may the year be crowned with many evidences of loving favor from the Fountain of all blessings.

But you and I know by experience that we very decidedly influence the course of our lives by our own deeds; and that is one reason why Solomon so persistently advised the seeking for wisdom, the wisdom that would make us wise enough to choose the things best for us. So often people choose inferior things, and move along lower levels, when they could live on higher levels with better thinking, happier and healthier exercise of all the faculties of body and mind.

The altruistic life, where one is steadily seeking the welfare of others has been proven by many to bring the sweetest joy, the happiest hours, the most contentment.

So, for 1920, let's you and I seek to develop the altruistic spirit as we strive to make all about us happy, we ourselves radiating cheerfulness. Never mind when you fail—try, and try again. You will find it really worthwhile.

And so we wish you all a very, very Happy New Year.

*Geo. D. Dayton*

In this December 1919 issue of *Daytonews*, greetings for the New Year from George Dayton also contained fatherly advice. From the first, Dayton enjoyed his role as patriarch to a large family of employees, who collectively called themselves "Daytonia." He and his wife, Emma Chadwick Dayton, often hosted dinners at home, inviting groups of employees. When the staff grew much larger, they instead hosted dinners in the tearooms. At Christmas, he and other members of top management stood at the door to offer each employee happy holidays and a box of candy.

A June 1919 *Daytonews* illustrated story depicts how a salesgirl can attain her dream of buyership. Working at Dayton's was a solid career path for women at a time when their choices were limited. Dayton's offered employees an education at their Commercial School, which in some cases began with the basics of arithmetic, spelling, and "deportment." The school offered courses in retail-related areas such as salesmanship and textiles, and added studies in history, geography, and composition. The three-year program was divided into three terms with two hours of classes each week, all under the control of Ima Winchell Stacy, the sister-in-law of Draper Dayton. Stacy also implemented glee clubs, men's clubs, and orchestras, which led to concerts and a variety of entertainments in the store.

In this 1910 photograph of the Dayton's women's wear department, the blouses are displayed on low, wide tables making it easy to fully view all that was available.

In the first decade of the 1900s, daylight flooded the space of Dayton's jewelry department. The store was built on the edges of residential Minneapolis, where there were few tall buildings to block the flow of light.

Dayton's tearooms served as many as 600 customers a day during the second decade of the 20th century and were open in the evenings for special banquets and dinner clubs. Dayton's goal was always to do its best to be "all things to all people," not wanting to leave any stone unturned when it came to customer satisfaction. Its three point program of service included providing a generous merchandising policy, capturing the customer's imagination with its goods, and preventing her (Dayton's always acknowledged its primary customers were women) from wandering to the competition with conveniences and attractions. First among these attractions were food and the tearooms.

In the second decade of the 20th century, linens and lingerie were kept in glass cases and boxes behind the counter. Customers were seated and sales clerks brought products to them, a typical arrangement for dry goods stores of the day. Dayton's was aware of the competition and always did its best to make the ordinary shopping experience something better by providing better service and higher quality. In 1909, customer convenience and satisfaction reached new levels when the Radisson Hotel opened up right next door, a development orchestrated by George Dayton himself.

Pictured here is the Dayton's second floor millinery in full bloom, around 1910. Women customarily wore hats in that era, and Dayton's displays them here on elegant, long-legged tables and inside tall, gleaming cabinetry.

In 1918, this Ladies Lounge (or Rest Room as it was known) at Dayton's provided a spacious retreat for women shoppers who often stayed for longer periods to read, write a letter, or simply relax. Dayton's also had an infirmary where employees and patrons could receive medical treatment from a full-time registered nurse. If customers grew hungry, they could go to one of the tearooms, or head to the downstairs store for a quick snack at the lunch counter. For men, a popular spot was the Men's Grill.

The furniture shown here is ornate, expensive, and for the customer of means. Around 1910, Dayton's home furnishings were always focused on the tastes of the sophisticated shopper, drawn to the rich fabrics and Italianate sculpting. This high-priced merchandise revealed Dayton's desire to appeal to everyone, regardless of income. Later the store opened the Dayton Company Studio, for the "discriminating buyer" of interior decoration and also added Spanish style furnishings. *Daytonews* reported that while the furnishings were somewhat at odds with American design, somehow the studio had managed to make the department look "homey."

This is Dayton's women's hosiery, fabrics, and notions department during the second decade of the 20th century. Chairs placed at long counters allowed customers to relax and let sales clerks show them new products or their requested items. Some of the items were bedding, silks, woolens, veiling, laces, ribbons, and knit undergarments.

Chic, yet proper dresses, blouses, and skirts were the Dayton's ideal from the very first days. Here in the women's wear department during the second decade of the 20th century, women and girls could find the best in well-made styles and enjoy Dayton's spacious, orderly presentation. The new 1913 annex included changes to the third floor, which the *Minneapolis Tribune* described as "the dream place for women. Nothing could be more elegant or diffuse and air of such utter luxury. Of mahogany woodwork of artistic and costly design there is no end, and treading the green velvet carpet is like strolling the golf links."

In this 1910 photograph, Dayton's decorates the fabrics and notions department during the holidays.

This 1917 Nicollet Avenue street scene shows Dayton's on the left.

THE DAYTON COMPANY.

This is Dayton's livery stable. Dayton's relied on Merchant's Package Delivery to bring purchases to customers before 1917, but after that, they had their own team of draft horses, with names such as Coalie, Pet, Pearl, and Florence, who often won ribbons at the Minnesota State Fair. Later trucks were used, but heavier loads were still transported by horse-drawn methods.

In 1910, table linens and other fabrics were sold at Dayton's in the newly remodeled Downstairs Store (formerly the basement store). By this time, Dayton's had expanded to all six floors of the original building and had taken over many of the leased departments, occupying 150,000 square feet of floor space.

This is the 1917 excavation site for the three-story building at the rear of Dayton's corner store, increasing the store's presence along Eighth Street. When completed, Dayton's was on three sides of the block, on Seventh and Eighth Streets and Nicollet Avenue.

# *Two*

# THE 1920s

In 1920, Dayton's historic flight from New York generated a storm of publicity. A poster display at the Minnesota History Center titled "Dayton's and the Jenny" describes the scene: "Pilot Ray Miller unloads merchandise in front of Dayton's store on Nicollet Avenue in Minneapolis, May 10, 1920. On his return from New York, Miller made a narrow escape. A rainstorm blinded him and his altitude dropped in line with 'a tree straight ahead of me. I zoomed up as hard as I could. . . . I brushed the branches.'" After the plane landed, its wings were removed and the pilot drove it downtown for this dramatic street-side delivery to Dayton's. (Courtesy of the Minnesota Historical Society.)

In 1923, crowds gathered at Dayton's Christmas window displays. Recognizing potential customers in children, Dayton's created display windows that would easily appeal to youth, often including a dramatic spectacle such as mechanical elephants. These were the years of the Ziegfeld Follies and Cecil B. DeMille, so expectations of spectacles were high. Dayton's windows accommodated with circus adventures and other themes based on familiar Christmas stories or movies.

It is a good day for a movie and a little shopping; Minneapolis is looking sleek on this rainy day in 1924 with Dayton's in the background. The Dayton Company at this time occupied 750,000 square feet of space in all its facilities. (Courtesy of the Minnesota Historical Society.)

In 1920, Dayton's models are waiting backstage at a State Theatre style show in full flapper-style evening wear, likely from the French room. Before the Oval Room, Dayton's guided customers to a "consistently high level of choice" when it created the French Room, which was stocked with haute couture from elite Paris fashion houses such as Lucien LeLong, Marcel Rochat, Jean Patou, Madeleine Vionnet, and Coco Chanel. Dayton's stylist (or buyer and fashion consultant) Marie Thompson Hill led the way. (Courtesy of the Minnesota Historical Society.)

Even though it would not have a department fully devoted to bridal costumes until the 1940s, in 1923, Dayton's could still fashionably outfit each member of the bridal party, including the bride, the maid of honor, the bride's maids, and the flower girl, all shown here in the display window.

Dayton's display window shows mannequins in the classic 1920s flapper silhouette, with loose fitting jackets, straight skirts, and exposed ankles.

With this classic 1920s art deco illustration, the Studio at Dayton's sells Porch and Cottage furniture, which captures the relaxed essence of life at the lakes.

In this 1922 Jubilee sale advertisement, finely rendered illustrations of children at school and at play promote "store-wide savings," and Minneapolis schools. *Daytonews* reported on the store's biggest day, "Jubilee! All kinds of predictions had been made to its outcome. But there was no one who predicted the true results. The sale went far over every quota, every previous figure, every expectation. And it didn't rain, snow or hail. Jubilee Day goes down in history."

Dayton's furs and fur-trimmed coats exude 1920s chic in this high-contrast store window display. "Furs" in Broadway typeface complete the art deco look.

Dayton's advertisement features Queentex Cotton Foulard fabrics for ready-to-wear dresses. Foulard is a sturdy, yet light-weight fabric made of weaved cotton or silk. Shown here is the true 1920s silhouette, with a flat bust line, dropped waist, and a bow on the side.

This Dayton's model is wearing a white 1920s evening dress, with a handkerchief hemline and fur-trim jacket. (Courtesy of the Minnesota Historical Society.)

These models from Dayton's line up for the 1920s style show at the State Theatre in Minneapolis. Bobbed hair and heavily made-up eyes complete the silhouette. (Courtesy of the Minnesota Historical Society.)

Here Dayton's advertises its 1928 World-Wide Exhibit, which was displayed in the windows along Nicollet Avenue. The display documented the progress of world trade through the advancement of science and its "thrilling conquest of the seas." The exhibit also was a celebration of new materials, simpler designs, respect for functionality, and use of color emerging from Czechoslovakia, the Phillipines, Mexico, India, and Europe.

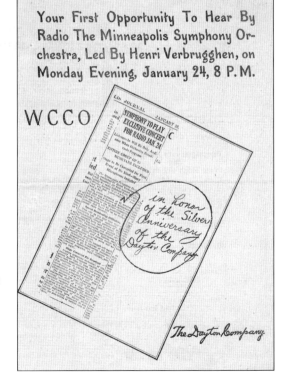

The Minneapolis Symphony Orchestra's first radio broadcast honored Dayton's silver anniversary in 1927. In 1926, George Dayton arranged for six concerts by the Minneapolis Symphony Orchestra to be broadcast over WCCO radio. Other than the New York Philharmonic broadcasts, it was the most expensive program of radio concerts ever undertaken.

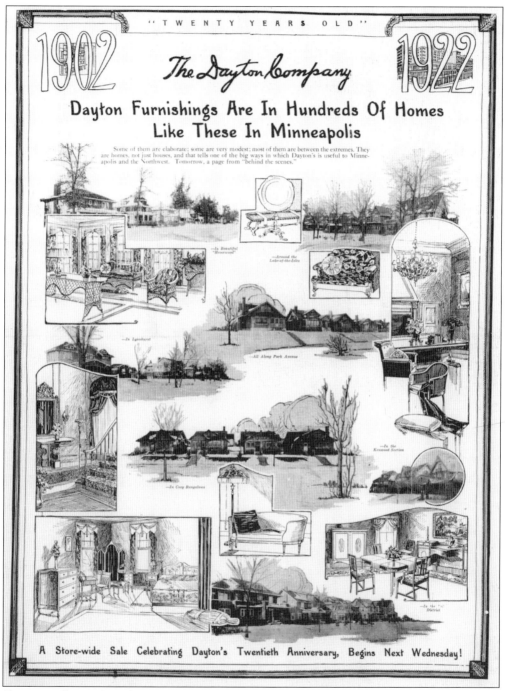

Shoppers of home furnishings enjoyed markdowns during the first Jubilee sale at Dayton's, which commemorated the store's 20th year in business.

These are issues of *Daytonews*, the news magazine for employees. The first issue appeared on July 10, 1918, and as print processes improved, so did the design of the magazine. Each issue reported company business followed by employee news, floor by floor. The fourth-floor news from May 1929 is typical: "Mr. Merriman of the Toy Department just returned from a three week trip to New York. We hear that he gave several people instructions in how to do group buying properly. . . . The girls of the Bridge Shop were entertained by Ilyron Langley at her home [includes exact address] on Friday, April 26th. The evening was spent playing bridge, after which Miss Langley announced her marriage to Mr. Richard Schall. . . . The book and picture departments were more than thrilled when they were honored with a visit from Florence Reed, guest star at the Shubert. Miss Reed went into raptures over our art galleries, and was heard to say that we have a most perfect atmosphere there, with the music from the Victrola department, and the lovely pictures."

In 1929, Dayton's remodeled its Looking Glass Salon. Rust, silver, and soft green shades were the color scheme, and the new carpet, chairs, lamps, and mirrors were selected from Dayton's own departments. The wood paneling was a combination of walnut with inlaid sections of harewood imported from Germany and Carpathian elm from Turkey. Parker's Scalp Treatments and facials were the only services available in this new section.

Here are members of the Radio Room Orchestra at the Dayton Company's radio station, WBAH. Dayton's was the first store in the area to use radio advertising. After a struggling start in 1922, WBAH was rebuilt and opened again in October 1923, later setting long distance records when broadcasts were heard in California, Mexico, Alaska, and England. (Courtesy of the Minnesota Historical Society.)

Dayton's offered a variety of enamel cast-iron stoves and ranges in the 1920s.

George Dayton greets a Curtiss Air delivery in 1920. In a publicity stunt, he had ordered pilots to deliver packages by air to customers who had purchased items at the Minnesota State Fair. The pilots delivered the goods to 24 Minnesota towns. Dayton was a neighbor of William Kidder, who owned the Curtiss-Northwest Airline. He often ran into him on his evening walks and the two men would discuss their business concerns. Soon after their discussions, Dayton devised this publicity event.

Dayton's models are shown here at Glenwood Chalet in 1925, looking chic and athletic in Dayton's winter wear and ski equipment from the store's new sporting goods department. Draper Dayton created the department in the mid-1920s, hiring ski instructors and outfitting the store with the appropriate equipment. (Courtesy of the Minnesota Historical Society.)

A man (perhaps a window dresser) applies makeup to a wax model in 1925. (Courtesy of the Minnesota Historical Society.)

In 1926, Dayton's opened its first exclusive men's department, which included two moose heads, perhaps easing the discomfort of the wary male shopper in an otherwise feminine domain. *Daytonews* described its design and effect, "as modern as the starchless stiff collar, as sparkling as a diamond shirt stud, and as practical as an elastic top sock; that briefly describes the spanking new layout in Dayton's Men's Furnishing Department. The dark walnut paneling sharply outlined in gleaming brass is a mellow background muting the brilliance of the case lights. The cubistic simplicity of the design and the trimness of cases, shelves, cash desks and counter openings suggest the speed and efficiency of a streamlined motorcar."

A 1920s Dayton Company billboard reminds travelers that the drive to Dayton's was a smooth ride on new pavement.

In 1920, Dayton's delivery would not be held up by Minnesota winters. Here sleigh delivery flows over the frozen waters of Lake Minnetonka, after a top section of a horse-drawn wagon was simply placed on runners. After World War I, Dayton's developed a full delivery service, claiming that in a single day of business, it could deliver "1000 carpet sweepers and 1000 potted palms."

In this Dayton's display window from the 1920s, formal evening wear is shown in new, fresh styles. This showed a dramatic change in fashion, which shifted at the beginning of World War I. The loose fitting dresses could be worn by anyone, doing away with the tailored, rigid formality of the upper-class silhouette.

In 1925, Dayton's joined the Norse Centennial Celebration, covering the entire store width on the Nicollet Avenue side with huge Norwegian and American flags. Dayton's display windows featured tributes to Norway's social life, history, and art. One window depicted the legend of Leif Ericson, another showed Norwegian craftwork in shawls, brass, and jewelry. Most dramatic was the window showing the launch of the Norwegian ship *Restaurationen* as it left Stavanger carrying the first group of emigrants from Norway to American shores.

In the late 1920s, Dayton's opened the University Branch. The three-story Elizabethan building located near the University of Minnesota campus was leased by Dayton's and employed 60 people, 50 of them students. The first floor was devoted to women's wear, second floor to men's, and the third floor was a tearoom called the Tent. A few years later, Dayton's opened a second restaurant next door called the Dungeon, directly appealing to male students. Former Minnesota governor Harold Stassen was an employee of the store during his law school days, eventually becoming a longtime friend of Nelson Dayton.

These art deco display windows provide a fitting backdrop for Dayton's 1920s dresses in the latest styles, showing bare arms, the new fashion statement.

This late 1920s display window was dedicated to the Minneapolis Auto Show. As described by the Dayton Company, "The large background panorama moved constantly, depicting the entire route from downtown Minneapolis to the Auto Show building. . . . Behind the cars at the curb a number of small cars on a chain drive track moving quite rapidly in front of the panorama lends a busy traffic effect to the entire scene."

These are Dayton's switchboard operators on the seventh floor in 1920. The June 10, 1920, *Daytonews* stated, "If someone were to tell you that 48 trunk lines run in and out of Daytonia, you might imagine that the store was a railroad station or that Mr. Lauer had so enlarged the Luggage Section that we carried that many lines of trunks. However, what we have in mind is the telephone switchboard equipment. Take it from us who have investigated, it is some equipment; just about as big as that used in a town of ten thousand people. . . . The next time you get impatient and jiggle the hook up and down to give vent to your feelings, come up on the 7th floor, and watch the girls operating the switchboard. Believe me Xantippe, it's enough to make the average person go crazy."

Pearl necklaces and flapper-style evening wear are shown in this 1920s window display. Fashion accessories were important to the flapper costume, especially the long pearl necklace and the cloche hat, shown here.

The Dayton's women's wear department in the 1920s had spacious aisles and strategically placed areas for resting tired feet, making the store a relaxing place to shop.

This stunning 1928 *Minneapolis Journal* illustration alerts Dayton's shoppers to their new parking garage. Parking was a problem in downtown Minneapolis, making shoppers think twice about making the trip. Dayton's resolved the conflict by building the new four-story garage at a cost of $500,000. It had a subbasement and a basement, and parking was just 75¢ for a 12-hour stay.

A car is seen here leaving Dayton's new garage in 1928.

## *Three*

# THE 1930S AND 1940S

In 1936, Dayton's autumn catalog celebrated 34 years of doing business in Minneapolis. This cover shows images of the main store and its many expansions in the background, which include the University of Minnesota campus store, the parking garage, and J. B. Hudson Jewelers, which Dayton's had purchased and moved under its roof in 1929.

# MINNEAPOLIS
## A Good Place To Live And Work

The new year has begun well. Business in quite a few lines is showing an increase in the first days of 1931. Savings are increasing. People are paying their debts on time.

—These are facts, proven by figures; not just generalizations intended to help us keep up our courage.

And 1930 was a year for Minneapolis to be proud of in many respects. In contrast to the discouraging news that came from other cities all over the United States, Minneapolis has been holding its own, or coming very close to it.

Unemployment, on which exact figures are being ascertained this week, appears to have been less here than in a great majority of our cities. Declines in those lines of business that found 1930 a hard year were less here than in most other cities —this includes retail store sales. Flour-making, one of our basic Minneapolis industries, showed almost no decline. Bank debits, an important barometer, declined here less than elsewhere.

Our Community Fund raised 19% over last year, against an average for 130 other cities of only 9.1% increase. And our delinquent taxes are less, in percentage, than in many other cities.

In Minneapolis, where by government figures the cost of living is always among the lowest of American cities—generally about 90% of the average—an important trade journal reports that retail commodity prices have been reduced 27% below last year.

Minneapolis ranked first in the seven cities of the United States showing an increase in postal receipts for December, 1930. And only these seven, out of 50, showed any increase.

—A good place to live, and to do business—A place that, with the splendid agricultural area back of it, never suffers as greatly as most cities from either over-inflation or under-inflation—Where conditions are more uniform, more inviting, more livable, than in many other communities.

The Dayton Company has had a year's business for which it is grateful, and is appreciative of the way the new year is starting. We are happy to be doing business in the Northwest rather than somewhere else. On the eve of our Twenty-ninth Anniversary Sale we congratulate you and ourselves that we are citizens "of no mean city."

*The Dayton Company.*

January 17, 1931.

Dayton's published a positive message about the Minneapolis business climate during the years of the Great Depression. Despite the financial outlook, Dayton's did not cut back but instead put more effort into keeping the business running well. They kept the same number of employees on the payroll and held the same store-wide sales, including Anniversary, Daisy, Jubilee, and Old Fashioned Bargain Days. Dayton's advertisements were decorated with large cornucopias, depicting tons of goods pouring forth from trucks and trains, which reflected the store's strength and will to affirm the positive.

In this 1930s image of Dayton's main floor, the rounded corners of the display cases and the cream-color ceilings against rich brown cabinetry beautify the surroundings on aisle nine.

The Sub-Deb Shop was designed for girls in their late teens, a unique marketing idea of Dayton's in the 1920s. The store adopted the term "subdeb" from author Mary Roberts Rinehart's series of stories about teenagers. Dayton's later generated a special line of dresses, called Dayne Taylor, named for the shop's innovators, Dayne Donovan and Charles Taylor.

On a hot day in 1938, it is "Air Cooled Inside" at Eighth Street and Nicollet Avenue.

Dayton's delivery drivers gather for a photograph with George Dayton (far left). The last teams of horses were retired in 1935 to Boulder Bridge, the Dayton family farm on Lake Minnetonka, and were replaced with trucks. By the 1950s, Dayton's had 11 delivery vehicles. (Courtesy of the Minnesota Historical Society.)

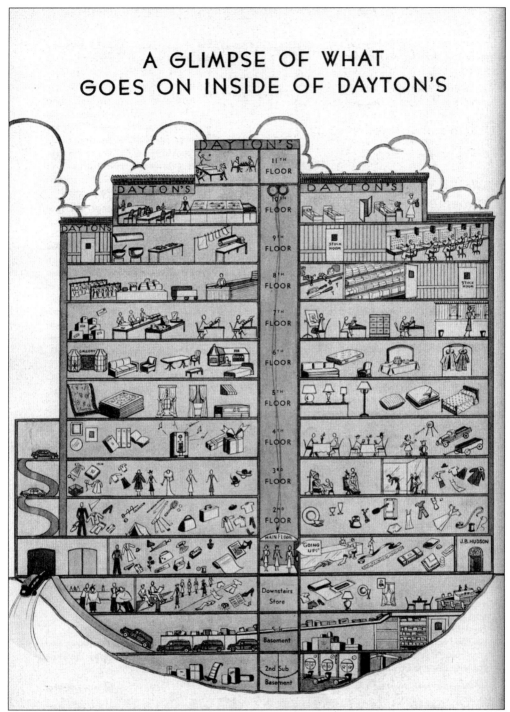

The autumn *Daytonian* of 1936 shows a cut-away illustration of all of Dayton's departments in the 1930s, beginning with the three basement levels. The sixth floor home furnishings department included a display house (model home), and on the other end of the same floor, a temperature-controlled vault was filled with summering furs.

(Left) Corner of the handsome Main Diningroom looking toward the Dinette.

(Below) The Lounge, where blond wood walls are satiny under concealed lighting, gives you your first glimpse of the Tea Rooms' modern beauty.

(Below) Corner of the wood panelled Men's Grill.

(First below) The stage as seen from the Banquet Room.
(Second below) Section of the many-windowed Dinette.

## The New TEA ROOMS

There are four important sections that make up the new Tea Rooms on the seventh floor:

The Main Diningroom, done in royal blue and blond maple, serves a full restaurant menu. It is an attractive place in which to entertain.

The Dinette, cheerful with many frosted windows and a color scheme of chartreuse and gold tones, specializes in salads, light lunches and fountain service.

The Men's Grill, with the masculine atmosphere of oak panelling and red leather, serves a menu suited to masculine tastes.

The Banquet Room, which can be shut off by sliding curtains, is for large assemblies. The absence of pillars in this room gives an unrestricted view of the stage.

A public address system carries Dick Long's orchestra music, or announcements to far corners.

20,000 square feet is the area covered by the new Tea Rooms. This, of course includes the kitchens and service quarters.

As modern as the Tea Rooms decorating is the equipment in the modern kitchen. Near at hand are the bakery and the candy kitchens.

All this combines to assure you delicious food, served efficiently in beautiful surroundings.

In the spring of 1938, the *Daytonian* reported on the store's new and expanded tearooms.

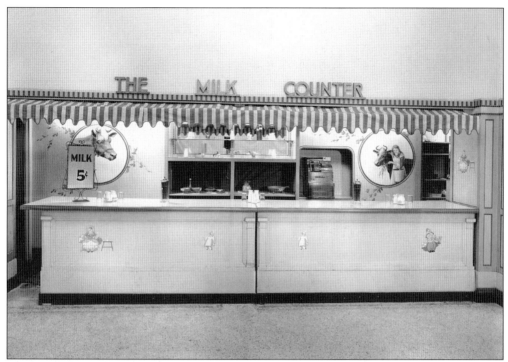

Fresh milk was 5 ¢ at Dayton's. It was one of many ways visitors could refresh themselves during a day of shopping in the 1930s.

Dayton's Christmas 1930s window display shows rows of dolls that delighted the hearts of little girls. The Shirley Temple doll at right was especially popular during the child actress's Hollywood reign during the 1930s.

Christmas on Nicollet Avenue in 1931 is pictured here. By the 1930s, Dayton's employed approximately 10,000 people, had 17 elevators, and had a telephone system that handled as much traffic as a city of 25,000.

In 1941, Dayton's autumn catalog delighted in the store's new streamlined escalators, marking the beginning of a major expansion that took place throughout the decade. Anticipating the installation, the *Minneapolis Times* reported, "The moving stairways will be four feet wide, which is ample for two persons to stand side by side, and will have a capacity to carry 4,000 people per hour between each two floors. There will be both up and down moving stairways, giving a total capacity at any one time of 12,000 per hour."

Dayton's had several store sports teams that competed with other merchant teams throughout the Twin Cities in baseball, basketball, bowling, and golf.

# A STORE'S ROLE IN WARTIME

There have been changes . . . the bride of yesterday is the coed of today, reversing the usual order . . . the spare room is occupied by the married daughter whose husband has answered the call, or by a defense worker . . . for some it is breakfast at night, sleep in the afternoon, play in the morning . . . priorities . . . price ceilings . . . the country at war! So much has been changed: nobody knows better than Dayton's how much has been changed. And there are more changes to come.

Our responsibility: To contribute to the war effort, of course, in any way that's genuine and sincere; but along the line of normal function to adjust our operations to face the changes . . . to depart from cut-and-dried formulae when it is to the public's best interest, as exemplified by our new Monday hours: 12 noon to 9 p. m. . . . to serve in THEIR way those whose lives have been disrupted . . . to impose no restrictions other than those which wartime regulations compel . . . to keep the public informed and up to date on changes affecting merchandise . . . to help protect our economic structure by full cooperation with efforts to hold prices in line . . . to maintain as long as possible standards of quality and value, resorting to substitutes only when necessary . . . and to perform whatever becomes our duty as earnestly as you in your homes and factories are holding America's Home Front.

*The Dayton Company*

In its 1942 autumn catalog, Dayton's describes the store's role in the war effort. *Daytonews* also included a Roll Call segment during the war, which provided updates on the whereabouts of enlisted employees. G. Nelson Dayton, who took over the store when George Dayton died, had five sons, four of whom were in the armed services during World War II: Bruce, Ken, Wallace, and Douglas. All were employees of the store, and their photographs in uniform appeared in the "Roll Call" section of the company newsletter in July 1945.

Dayton's sold armed services supplies during the 1940s. The company sent 314 men and women into the army, navy, and air force, and each was guaranteed a job upon their return home. Since many materials, such as metal and nylon, were needed for the war effort, several products were either no longer sold or taken from the shelves. In October 1942, there was a scrap metal drive for weaponry, and Dayton's sent workmen to the roof to dismantle its big electrical sign, which had long been a fixture in Minneapolis's growing skyline.

Dayton's designers pulled out all the stops to create the theme of the Broadway musical *Showboat* for this Minneapolis Aquatennial festival float. Dayton's employees competed in the Queen of the Lakes contest and often won the crown. Dayton's joined with Hudson's to design the queen's crown, made of sterling silver and plated in 24-karat gold, with jewels designed by William Hobe, an internationally-known gem designer.

This is Dayton's Eighth Street addition, which began construction in 1946. Leaving only the original structure at Nicollet Avenue and Seventh Street, the Eighth Street project raised the rest of the store to 12 stories. Air conditioning was added to all floors, and escalators were added up to the seventh floor. Nelson Dayton commented on the project for the *Minneapolis Times*, "We are trying to give Minneapolis as good a store as is furnished any city in the United States." Completed in 1948, the total cost was $1,550,000.

In this 1945 picture, Dayton's Oval Room shoppers admire a chic suit on display at the entrance of the room. The Oval Room started out as a department for "better dresses" called the Model Room. Per the store's expansion in the 1940s, it evolved into the Oval Room. The Oval Room achieved its popularity initially by bringing in the collections of American designer Gilbert Adrian, known simply as Adrian, who achieved fame creating broad-shouldered designs for Joan Crawford and bias-cut dresses for Jean Harlow—designs that he later developed for ready-to-wear fashion.

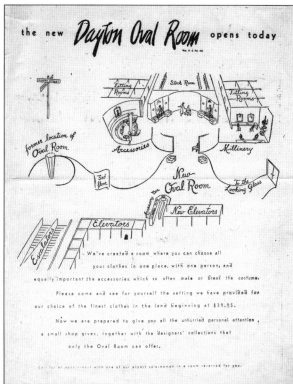

the new *Dayton Oval Room* opens today

former location of Oval Room.

3rd floor

Pioneer Street

Fitting Rooms

Stock Room

Fitting Rooms

Accessories

Millinery

New Oval Room

To the Looking Glass

Escalator

Elevators

Treasure Box

New Elevators

We've created a room where you can choose all your clothes in one place, with one person, and equally important the accessories, which so often make or break the costume.

Please come and see for yourself the setting we have provided for our choice of the finest clothes in the land beginning at $39.95.

Now we are prepared to give you all the unhurried personal attention a small shop gives, together with the designers' collections that only the Oval Room can offer.

Call for an appointment with one of our expert saleswomen in a room reserved for you.

Here Dayton's advertises the opening of the newly remodeled Oval Room in 1947, which was one among a succession of shops on the third floor. A New York retail publication reported, "The [third floor] shops adjoin each other by means of a long carpeted lane, featuring black plum walls and lighted by individual shops along the lane. This treatment gives the customer the feeling of entering a specialty store when she steps into one of the shops, and is reminiscent of the famous little couture shops of Paris."

Shown in this 1949 picture, the 12th floor powder room near the entrances of the Oak Grille and Sky Room provided a row of lighted vanities opposite a graceful arched hallway. Dayton's never forgot the importance of atmosphere.

This is the entrance to the Bride's Bureau. After an employee fully analyzed the local market by interviewing local citizens about religious customs and unique wedding ceremonies, Dayton's opened its first department devoted entirely to bridal dressing in the 1940s. Using a scrapbook filled with great detail, the employee made the argument to Nelson Dayton that Dayton's needed a full bridal department. Her suggestion blossomed into the Bride's Bureau, and she became its buyer.

The Oak Grille, Dayton's 12th-floor restaurant, is still in operation today. Leather upholstery and oak paneling evoke a club atmosphere in this 1947 photograph.

Portrait of a Civilian

This men's store advertisement shows the men's suit style of the 1930s and 1940s. Nelson Dayton gave new direction to the store when he introduced the men's store in August 1926. He hired a buyer from New York and completely remodeled the area where it was installed. Store trade names such as Dorville and Hoxton were established at this time.

# *Four*

# THE 1950S

In this 1952 collage showing the Dayton Company's storefronts and warehouses, Dayton's visually documents its growth. An image of Westminster Presbyterian church is in the upper left corner, which once stood at the southwest corner of Nicollet Avenue and Seventh Street. When the church burned to the ground, George Dayton bought the property and constructed the six-story building, which later became Dayton's department store.

**Maurice Rentner**

The monastic look —
with 1950's flattering,
feminine rounded
lines . . . its single
dramatic spring accent,
a fresh crisp linen yoke.

$110

*the Dayton Oval Room*

This Dayton's Oval Room advertisement from the 1950s shows the classic slim silhouette of the era. Here is a dress by American designer Maurice Rentner from the spring collection. Oval Room manager Jeanne Auerbacher once wrote, "In an Oval Room dress, one does not enter, one makes an entrance."

In their Easter Sunday best, a mother and daughter team of mannequins are looking proper in the 1940s, a fitting scene within Dayton's decorative arrangement of flowers and trees.

During Dayton's annual Jubilee sale, tables and counters were filled with marked-down goods, drawing crowds of mostly women who, in the 1940s and 1950s, always dressed up for a day of shopping.

In this clever 1950s graphic, Dayton's advertising department maximizes the Bali brand name with a touch of exotic fun.

take it

from a

Bali girl.

This Dayton's display window shows mannequins draped in fox stoles, full skirts, and slim sheath dresses of the late 1950s. Glamour and the luxury of furs were back, contrasting the austerity of the 1940s when materials for clothing were scarce.

Marion Manning, Miss America 1957, makes an appearance at Dayton's in downtown Minneapolis to a packed house.

This is Dayton's lingerie department on the fourth floor in the 1950s. Items of lingerie were on racks, or, as the tradition was in years past, retrieved from drawers and presented to shoppers by clerks who described their features in detail. Pastel decor and chandeliers created an atmosphere of feminine elegance.

This is the linens department at Dayton's around 1950, where women could find patterns and a wide selection of quality fabrics for dresses and separates.

At Dayton's, high style in women's fashion moved forward with technology into the 1950s. This display window reflects the optimism of the era with its new inventions, culture of leisure, and consumerism. Weekly cocktail parties created new reasons to be dressed up, and television played a big role in promoting it.

"Summer blossoms out in white" in Dayton's seventh floor furniture department, featuring 1950s-style white chairs, white geometric floor coverings, and a blonde wood table.

In 1955, Dayton's Marvelous Minnesota theme promoted summer clothing, family vacations, station wagons, fishing resorts, and camping. Pool parties were popular in the 1950s, which required special attention to fashionable swimwear. (Courtesy of the Minnesota Historical Society.)

In this Marvelous Minnesota display window of the 1950s, Dayton's promotes Minnesota vacations and summertime ready-to-wear.

This Dayton's advertisement for Jantzen illustrates how the structural support of undergarments has made all the difference in swimwear.

Here Dayton's employees review their work at the printing press in the 1950s. Dayton's established its own advertising department in the 1950s and added a printing press for weekly mailings and promotions.

A main floor spring fashion display in February 1957 anticipates a shift in seasons with blossoming branches and spring clothing, a welcome sight on cold winter days that often extend into April.

A selection of men's clothing is sold on Dayton's main floor in 1957.

Spring has arrived on Dayton's 1957 main floor, where ceilings and columns are draped with branches.

California Fiesta was a summer promotion of the 1950s. Featured here is a spandex one-piece bathing suit. Spandex fabric, with its ability to hold its shape when wet or dry, changed the bathing suit industry during the 1950s and 1960s.

In this 1958 Oval Room window display, mannequins in cocktail dresses share the spotlight with images of beautiful cars. Throughout the 1950s, Dayton's windows projected the new decade of the good life, leaving the war years decisively in the past.

Here are Dayton's shoppers during the winter, perhaps at Christmastime, on the main floor of the store in the 1950s.

Like many other local businesses during the 1950s, Dayton's had a presence at the Minnesota State Fair, but discontinued it in later years.

Dayton's updated its Nicollet Avenue plaque in the 1950s to reflect the new style of the company's logo.

Team member publications changed names over the years, sometimes even sharing a name with Dayton's advertising publications, like the *Daytonian*. The first employee publication was *Daytonews*, which began in 1918 but ceased for a time after the death of George Dayton in 1938. It reappeared again in 1945.

In this display window, Dayton's promotes a "Hi-Fi Music Festival," and the store's latest products in sound technology during the 1950s, a time when high fidelity stereo consoles were a part of every American living room.

Dayton's window advertises No-Mend Nylons, a new design in hosiery.

In 1955, Dayton's advertises its annual Jubilee sale with "Store-Wide Savings," featuring evening wear separates.

Now a thing of the past, For-Men-Only shops were a common sight in department stores around Christmastime. They were created for men who needed a little help finding gifts for the women in their lives.

Dayton's New World of Stereo offered Magnavox television and stereo consoles. Similar to radios of the 1930s and 1940s, consoles were a piece of living room furniture. Dayton's seventh-floor home furnishings department displayed them along with their couches and chairs.

In this 1955 image of Dayton's Sky Room restaurant, elaborate chandeliers grace the ceilings in an otherwise sparse decor.

The Sky Room was redecorated in 1951, and the walls were painted in this modern art style.

This is a Dayton's advertisement for the annual Daisy Sale that occurred each June. It was originally called simply "the Mid-Year sale," but was renamed "the Daisy Sale" in 1928 and remained so for the remainder of the store's life. Early on, Dayton's had adopted a pattern of stock reduction and liquidating high-priced items, which gave them an edge when the competition did not follow suit. In 1928, the volume of business was 27 times what it was after its first year.

An Oval Room display advertises Barbara Lee floral-print dresses, featuring straight line and bouffant-style skirts. The Oval Room always advertised separately from the other departments at Dayton's, creating a distinctive identity and profile of its own.

This is Dayton's Oval Room in the 1950s. The reception area was oval in shape, and the department's sleek decor complemented the clean lines of the decade's better fashions, ones of conservative elegance. The Oval Room carried designs of American designers such as Phillip Mangone, Hattie Carnegie, and Nettie Rosenstein, who was known as the "mother of the little black dress." Annual style shows brought these fashions to the public and often were sponsored by the Women's Auxiliary of Hennepin County and the Friends of the Institute.

This is what Christmas on Eighth Street in Minneapolis looked like in 1954. Dayton's Christmas decorations and city holiday lights combined to make a festive urban night.

*Five*

# THE 1960S

In its August 22, 1966, issue, *Newsweek* wrote, "The swingingest spot in Minneapolis? Well to hear the folks at Dayton's tell it, it's right by the dishpans and ironing boards, and just left of the wicker rockers-in Dayton's auditorium. This week the 1,500 seat auditorium is in the middle of a month long explosion in sound, billed 'Super Youthquake,' with the tremors supplied by such groups as the Yardbirds, Simon and Garfunkel, the Mitchell Trio and thousands of their frenetic fans . . . to general manager Kenneth Dayton, they all produce the same sweet sound: clanging cash registers." Youthquake was one of six shows that Dayton's put on yearly, at a cost of $30,000 to $50,000 each. (Courtesy of the Minneapolis Library archives.)

London scenes took over Dayton's eighth floor auditorium in 1966, so that shoppers might experience a stroll through Charles Dickens's "Merry Olde Englande at Christmastime."

The passion for Santa Bear was at times extreme, especially when he was first introduced at Christmas in 1985. A front page article in *DHDSC Today* (the Dayton Hudson Department Store Company employee magazine) explains, "While we've always maintained that the customer votes with her purse, we didn't expect this . . . when our Northland [Hudson's] store ran out of Santa Bears one irate woman wound up and smacked Store Manager Dennis Toffolo over the head." In the St. Paul Store, the dwindling supply of bears brought out more contentious behavior. "While one woman waited in line to purchase her Santa Bear, another approached from behind, grabbed the bear out of her arms, and disappeared behind racks of clothing with her kidnapped bear in tow."

In 1966, Dayton's-Bachman's Spring Flower Show turned the eighth floor auditorium into a paradise for the benefit of store business and winter-weary Minnesotans, each year drawing thousands of visitors downtown. The Dayton's-Bachman's partnership began in 1964, and became an annual tradition that continued for over 30 years.

In 1960, spring flowers engulfed the display cases of Dayton's main floor. On the theme of "A Plantation Garden of the Southern United States," 100,000 blooms filled the store.

A Dayton's spring flower show sign lights up the night in downtown Minneapolis in the 1960s.

In 1965, Dayton's showcased fashion leaders Andre Courreges and Roger Nelson, who brought minimalist clothing and London mod to Dayton's.

In this pop art window display, Dayton's features the latest styles of the anything-goes 1960s, including bold prints, leather jumpers, and pastel hose. Pop art music posters completed the image, showing Dayton's eye for trends and its desire to reach the youth-driven market.

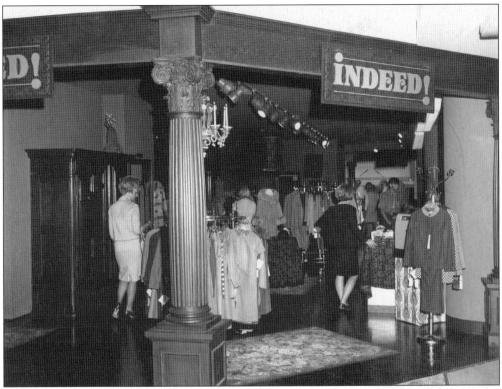

This is one of Dayton's many in-store boutiques, featuring the latest in upscale 1960s styles. (Right, courtesy of the Minneapolis Library archives.)

INDEED!

London op . . .
this pantsuit

On top . . . . op! It's
black and white and
checked all over.
Then bullseye buttoned.
And worn over pants
solidly black.
Fashion Indeed. $2.00.
3rd Floor Downtown.

Grandmother's Attic featured granny prints and granny dresses (tiny prints, lace trims, and rows of buttons) that were popular during the 1960s, alongside more traditional items for a creative mix.

In this Dayton's advertisement from 1965, the empire dress is shown in woolen fabrics ideal for Minnesota winters.

Items from the Out of Sight shops at Dayton's were in the display windows along Nicollet Avenue, lending them a 1960s-style edge. The Out of Sight shops were Dayton's homage to 1960s funkiness and the popularity of boutiques. Pop art posters, unusual light fixtures, and candle kitsch were mixed in with the anything-but-traditional clothes.

The Oval Room featured Rudi Gernreich beachwear, whose futuristic clothing designs played a key role in 1960s fashion. He was the first to use plastic, as shown here with these shiny thigh-high boots, which are a potent lime-green. Dayton's pushed its conservative image a bit when it carried Gernreich's topless swimsuit.

This is the entrance to the London mod fashion show, one of several during the 1960s when British influence dominated the fashion scene.

Pictured here is Dayton's leather department in 1968. Leather garments exploded on the fashion scene during the 1960s.

Brides hover like angels over the fountain near the Eighth Street entrance in 1968.

A display of ladies undergarments is from a time when girdles were a standard part of women's dressing, even for teenagers.

Bold graphics in a 1960s Jubilee sale display window are in letters large enough to read while driving by.

This is an advertisement for Dayton's 61st anniversary sale in 1963.

A mother and daughter have a moment together in Dayton's toy department in the 1960s.

In this display window, Dayton's promotes the Shelton Stroller, a popular, easy-care dress of the late 1950s and early 1960s. Stroller advertisements dubbed it as "the World's Most Practical Beautiful Dress."

Big crowds gather in downtown Minneapolis, decorated for Christmas. Many families made the trip downtown with their children just to see Dayton's display windows, which always had child-friendly themes. Here the store decorations merge with the city's, turning night into day.

Dayton's captures the playful attitude of 1960s fashion with this Plaza 8 lingerie advertisement, with floating models and op art graphics in green, purple, and turquoise.

How short is too short? Each person must decide their own best length, Dayton's says, in this July *Minneapolis Tribune* advertisement. (Courtesy of the Minneapolis Library archives.)

Showing the influence of the British invasion, Dayton's brought English model Twiggy to the Minneapolis store, and the event sold out. Twiggy was a fashion idol who was as popular among fashion-crazed teenaged girls as the Beatles were during the 1960s.

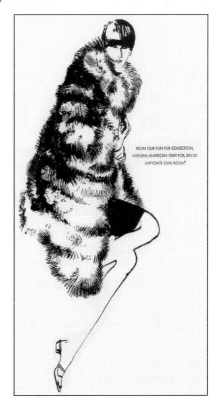

Dayton's Oval Room gets into the fun of the decade with fake fur in 1965. (Courtesy of the Minneapolis Library archives.)

This 1965 Dayton's display window created drama with contrasting lights and Paris geometrics, shown here in wool. Geometric patterns in clothing reflected popular art of the 1960s.

This Dayton's advertisement from the fall of 1968 shows a colorfully rendered fortune-teller in the style of famed 1960s artist Peter Max. The psychedelic graphics with a "blow your mind" aesthetic are a nod to the 1960s generation of free spirits.

These children are having breakfast with Santa in the Sky Room at Dayton's around 1940. (Courtesy of the Minnesota Historical Society.)

This is a fashion show in the Sky Room in the late 1940s. (Courtesy of the Minnesota Historical Society.)

Alexander Calder's *The Spinner,* is shown here on Nicollet Avenue near the store in the 1960s. Owned by Dayton's, it was eventually donated to Minneapolis's Walker Art Center in 1971.

*Six*

# THE 1970S AND BEYOND

This Minneapolis street scene shows Dayton's in the background.

Dayton's second floor video wall display in the 1980s shows the newly built Lake Harriet Band Shell and women on a stroll.

This is the entrance to Marketplace at 700 Under the Mall as it looked in 1978. Marketplace sold a variety of items for the kitchen and a wide range of foods from their deli. It also had a McGlynn's Bakery, a Leeann Chin's takeout, and the 700 Express Restaurant.

Mr. Shirley shops at Dayton's warehouse sale.

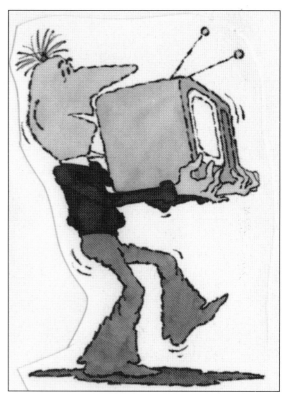

Rive Gauche was one of Dayton's specialty shops during the 1970s, featuring designer clothing by Yves Saint Laurent.

This is the entrance to the Minneapolis store's Oval Room of the 1970s, still home to high-end ready-to-wear clothing from American designers Ralph Lauren and Calvin Klein, as well as European couture.

Seen here is Paddington Station, home of the Paddington Bear at Christmas in 1976. Paddington Bear was the creation of English author Michael Bond, who featured the bear in his children's books.

The Investors Diversified Services (IDS) building in the background shares a photograph with Dayton's. The two were icons of 20th century Minneapolis.

Six plates show the changing designs of Dayton's store credit cards, beginning with the metal of Dayton Dry Goods to the 1990s green plastic of pre–Marshall Field's.

*Dimensions* was a team-member publication from the 1980s during Dayton's last years.

This street scene near Dayton's at Seventh Street and Nicollet Avenue was taken in the 1990s.

This portrait of George Dayton was made when he was 76 years old.

# ACROSS AMERICA, PEOPLE ARE DISCOVERING SOMETHING WONDERFUL. *THEIR HERITAGE.*

Arcadia Publishing is the leading local history publisher in the United States. With more than 3,000 titles in print and hundreds of new titles released every year, Arcadia has extensive specialized experience chronicling the history of communities and celebrating America's hidden stories, bringing to life the people, places, and events from the past. To discover the history of other communities across the nation, please visit:

## www.arcadiapublishing.com

Customized search tools allow you to find regional history books about the town where you grew up, the cities where your friends and family live, the town where your parents met, or even that retirement spot you've been dreaming about.